WILDLIFE SANCTUARIES

Wisconsin Ecoregions

- North Central Hardwood Forests
- Southeastern Wisconsin Till Plains
- Driftless Area
- Northern Lakes and Forests
- Western Corn Belt Plains
- Central Corn Belt Plains

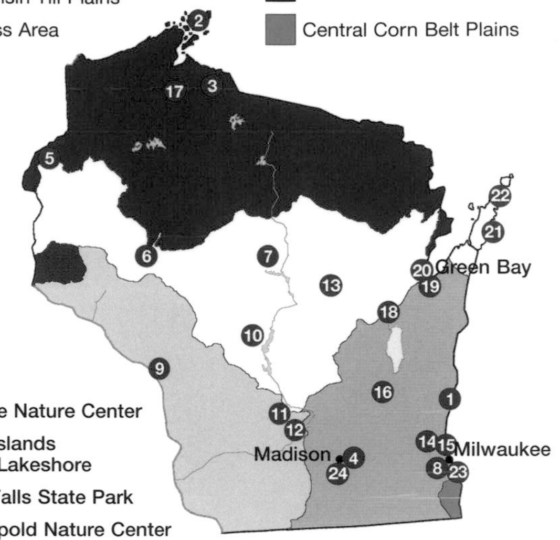

1. Riveredge Nature Center
2. Apostle Islands National Lakeshore
3. Copper Falls State Park
4. Aldo Leopold Nature Center
5. Crex Meadows Wildlife Area
6. Beaver Creek Reserve
7. George W. Mead Wildlife Area
8. Wehr Nature Center
9. Trempealeau National Wildlife Refuge (NWR)
10. Necedah NWR
11. Baxter's Hollow State Natural Area
12. Devil's Lake State Park
13. University of Wisconsin – Museum of Natural History
14. Havenwoods State Forest Environmental Awareness Center
15. Schlitz Audubon Nature Center
16. Horicon Marsh NWR
17. Cable Museum of Natural History
18. Gordon Bubolz Nature Preserve
19. Bay Beach Wildlife Sanctuary
20. L.H. Barkhausen Waterfowl Preserve
21. Whitefish Dunes State Park
22. Mink River Estuary State Natural Area
23. Milwaukee Public Museum
24. Madison Arboretum

Most illustrations show the adult male in breeding coloration. Colors and markings may be duller or absent during different seasons. The measurements denote the length of animals from nose/bill to tail tip. Butterfly measurements denote wingspan. Illustrations are not to scale.

Made in the USA

Waterford Press publishes reference guides to nature observation, outdoor recreation and survival skills. Product information is featured on the website: **www.waterfordpress.com**

To order or for information on custom published products please call 800-434-2555 or email orderdesk@waterfordpress.com. For permissions or to share comments email editor@waterfordpress.com.

ISBN 978-1-58355-614-6 $7.95 U.S.
9 781583 556146 50795
UPC 8 84682 01150 5
10 9 8 7 6 5 4 3 2 1 218224

WISCONSIN WILDLIFE – A Folding Pocket Guide to Familiar Animals

Kavanagh/Leung

A POCKET NATURALIST® GUIDE

WISCONSIN WILDLIFE

A Folding Pocket Guide to Familiar Animals

BUTTERFLIES & MOTHS

Black Swallowtail
Papilio polyxenes
To 3.5 in. (9 cm)

Orange Sulphur
Colias eurytheme
To 2.5 in. (6 cm)

Underwings
Silver-spotted Skipper
Epargyreus clarus
To 2.5 in. (6 cm)
Has a large, irregular silver patch on the underside of its hindwings. Patch is absent on the forewings.

Buckeye
Junonia coenia
To 2.5 in. (6 cm)
Note orange wing bars on forewings and eight distinct "eyespots."

Red Admiral
Vanessa atalanta
To 2.5 in. (6 cm)
Note orange bars on forewings and border of hindwings.

Cabbage White
Pieris rapae
To 2 in. (5 cm)
One of the most common butterflies.

Spring Azure
Celastrina ladon
To 1.3 in. (3.6 cm)
One of the earliest spring butterflies.

Baltimore Checkerspot
Euphydryas phaeton
To 2.5 in. (6 cm)

American Snout
Libytheana carinenta
To 2 in. (5 cm)
"Snout" is formed from projecting mouth parts which enclose its coiled proboscis.

Mourning Cloak
Nymphalis antiopa
To 3.5 in. (9 cm)

Eastern Tiger Swallowtail
Papilio glaucus
To 6 in. (15 cm)

Eastern Tailed Blue
Everes comyntas
To 1 in. (3 cm)
Note orange spots above thread-like hindwing tails.

Monarch
Danaus plexippus
To 4 in. (10 cm)
Note rows of white spots on edges of wings.

Question Mark
Polygonia interrogationis
To 2.5 in. (6 cm)
Note lilac margin on wings. Silvery mark on underwings resembles a question mark or semi-colon.

Luna Moth
Actias luna
To 4.5 in. (11 cm)

INVERTEBRATES

Bumble Bee
Bombus spp.
To 1 in. (3 cm)
Stout, furry bee is large and noisy.

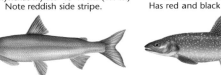

Crane Fly
Tipula spp.
To 2.5 in. (6 cm)
Slender fly has a long abdomen and long legs.

Ebony Jewelwing
Calopteryx maculata
To 2 in. (5 cm)
A damselfly, it rests with its wings folded over its back.

Field Cricket
Gryllus pennsylvanicus
To 1 in. (3 cm)
Shrill call is a series of 3 chirps.

Black Widow Spider
Latrodectus mactans
To .3 in. (8 mm)
Black spider is easily recognized by its shiny, bulbous abdomen with a red hourglass marking beneath. Venom can be lethal to children.

Water Boatman
Family Corixidae
To .5 in. (1.3 cm)

Paper Wasp
Polistes spp.
To 1 in. (3 cm)
Builds papery hanging nests. Can sting repeatedly.

Green Darner
Anax junius
To 3 in. (8 cm)
Has a bright green thorax and a blue body. Rests with its wings open.

Migratory Grasshopper
Melanoplus sanguinipes
To 1.5 in. (4 cm)

Wolf Spider
Family Lycosidae
To 1.5 in. (4 cm)
Has 8 eyes arranged in 3 rows. Most do not weave webs but catch prey by pouncing on it.

Northern Walkingstick
Diapheromera femorata
To 4 in. (10 cm)
Stick-like insect stays camouflaged among twigs.

Honey Bee
Apis mellifera
To .75 in. (2 cm)
Slender bee can sting only once.
Wisconsin's state insect.

Black Horse Fly
Tabanus atratus
To 1.25 in. (3.2 cm)
Note large head. Females feed on blood and deliver painful bites. Similar deerflies have dark-patterned wings.

Widow Skimmer
Libellula luctuosa
To 2 in. (5 cm)
Dragonfly has broad white bands across its mid-wings.

Black-and-yellow Garden Spider
Argiope aurantia
To 1.25 in. (3.2 cm)

Water Strider
Gerris spp.
To .5 in. (1.3 cm)
Long-legged insect skates along the surface of the water.

GAME FISHES

Rainbow Trout
Oncorhynchus mykiss To 44 in. (1.1 m)
Note reddish side stripe.

Lake Whitefish
Coregonus clupeaformis
To 30 in. (75 cm)
Note concave forehead.

Largemouth Bass
Micropterus salmoides To 40 in. (1 m)
Jaw joint extends beyond the eye.

Muskellunge
Esox masquinongy To 6 ft. (1.8 m)
Prized sport fish is an aggressive predator.
Wisconsin's state fish.

Northern Pike
Esox lucius To 53 in. (1.4 m)

Yellow Perch
Perca flavescens To 16 in. (40 cm)
Note 6-9 dark "saddles" down its side.

White Bass
Morone chrysops To 18 in. (45 cm)
Silvery fish has 4-7 dark side stripes.

Channel Catfish
Ictalurus punctatus To 4 ft. (1.2 m)

Brown Trout
Salmo trutta To 40 in. (1 m)
Has red and black spots on its body.

Lake Trout
Salvelinus namaycush To 4 ft. (1.2 m)

White Crappie
Pomoxis annularis To 20 in. (50 cm)

Pumpkinseed
Lepomis gibbosus To 16 in. (40 cm)

Bluegill
Lepomis macrochirus To 16 in. (40 cm)

Smallmouth Bass
Micropterus dolomieu To 27 in. (68 cm)
Jaw joint is beneath the eye.

Walleye
Sander vitreus To 40 in. (1 m)
Note dark blotch on rear of first dorsal fin and white spot on lower lobe of tail.

Lake Sturgeon
Acipenser fulvescens To 8 ft. (2.4 m)
Note elongate snout and bumps down its back.

REPTILES & AMPHIBIANS

Red Eft
Eastern Newt
Notophthalmus viridescens To 6 in. (15 cm)
Juvenile called an "eft" is red-orange.

Tiger Salamander
Ambystoma tigrinum
To 13 in. (33 cm)

American Toad
Anaxyrus americanus
To 4.5 in. (11 cm)

Chorus Frog
Pseudacris triseriata
To 1.5 in. (4 cm)
Note dark stripes on back. Call sounds like running a thumbnail over the teeth of a comb.

Northern Leopard Frog
Lithobates pipiens
To 4 in. (10 cm)
Brown to green frog has dark spots on its back. Call is a rattling snore.

Bullfrog
Lithobates catesbeianus
To 8 in. (20 cm)
Call is a deep-pitched – *jug-o-rum*.

Western Painted Turtle
Chrysemys picta bellii
To 10 in. (25 cm)

Snapping Turtle
Chelydra serpentina To 18 in. (45 cm)
Note knobby shell and long tail.

Milk Snake
Lampropeltis triangulum triangulum
To 7 ft. (2.1 m)

Smooth Green Snake
Opheodrys vernalis
To 26 in. (65 cm)

Ringneck Snake
Diadophis punctatus
To 30 in. (75 cm)

Eastern Fox Snake
Pantherophis gloydi
To 6 ft. (1.8 m)

Northern Water Snake
Nerodia sipedon To 4.5 ft. (1.4 m)
Note dark blotches on back.

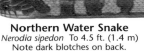

Common Garter Snake
Thamnophis sirtalis sirtalis
To 4 ft. (1.2 m)
Green, brown or black snake has yellowish back stripes.

Timber Rattlesnake
Crotalus horridus To 6 ft. (1.8 m)
Found in SW Wisconsin and along Mississippi and Wisconsin rivers.

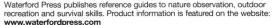

Canada Goose
Branta canadensis
To 45 in. (1.14 m)

Winter
Summer

Common Loon
Gavia immer
To 3 ft. (90 cm)

American Coot
Fulica americana
To 16 in. (40 cm)

Pied-billed Grebe
Podilymbus podiceps
To 13 in. (33 cm)
Note banded white bill.

Double-crested Cormorant
Phalacrocorax auritus
To 3 ft. (90 cm)

Wood Duck
Aix sponsa
To 20 in. (50 cm)

Blue-winged Teal
Spatula discors To 16 in. (40 cm)

Mallard
Anas platyrhynchos To 28 in. (70 cm)

Great Egret
Ardea alba
To 38 in. (95 cm)
Note yellow bill and black feet.

Green Heron
Butorides virescens
To 22 in. (55 cm)

Sandhill Crane
Antigone canadensis
To 4 ft. (1.2 m)

Great Blue Heron
Ardea herodias
To 4.5 ft. (1.4 m)

Killdeer
Charadrius vociferus
To 12 in. (30 cm)
Note two breast bands.

Ring-billed Gull
Larus delawarensis
To 20 in. (50 cm)
Bill has dark ring.

Herring Gull
Larus argentatus
To 26 in. (65 cm)
Legs are pinkish.

Mourning Dove
Zenaida macroura
To 13 in. (33 cm)
Call is a mournful –
ooah-woo-woo-woo.

Rock Pigeon
Columba livia
To 13 in. (33 cm)

Belted Kingfisher
Megaceryle alcyon
To 14 in. (35 cm)

Northern Flicker
Colaptes auratus
To 13 in. (33 cm)
Wing and tail linings are yellow.

Red-headed Woodpecker
Melanerpes erythrocephalus
To 10 in. (25 cm)

Downy Woodpecker
Dryobates pubescens
To 6 in. (15 cm)
The similar hairy woodpecker is larger and has a longer bill.

Turkey Vulture
Cathartes aura
To 32 in. (80 cm)
Note red head and two-toned underwings.

Red-tailed Hawk
Buteo jamaicensis
To 25 in. (63 cm)

American Kestrel
Falco sparverius
To 12 in. (30 cm)

Osprey
Pandion haliaetus
To 2 ft. (60 cm)

Bald Eagle
Haliaeetus leucocephalus
To 40 in. (1 m)

Barred Owl
Strix varia
To 2 ft. (60 cm)
Call is a loud –
who-cooks-for-you?
who-cooks-for-you-all?

Great Horned Owl
Bubo virginianus
To 25 in. (63 cm)
Call is a resonant –
hoo-HOO-hoooo.

Ruby-throated Hummingbird
Archilochus colubris
To 3.5 in. (9 cm)

Great Crested Flycatcher
Myiarchus crinitus
To 9 in. (23 cm)

Tree Swallow
Tachycineta bicolor
To 6 in. (15 cm)

Common Nighthawk
Chordeiles minor
To 10 in. (25 cm)
Often hawks for insects around street lights.

Purple Martin
Progne subis
To 8 in. (20 cm)

Common Grackle
Quiscalus quiscula
To 14 in. (35 cm)

Eastern Kingbird
Tyrannus tyrannus
To 8 in. (20 cm)
Note broad white tail band.

American Crow
Corvus brachyrhynchos
To 22 in. (55 cm)
Call is a distinct – caw.

Horned Lark
Eremophila alpestris
To 8 in. (20 cm)

Brown-headed Cowbird
Molothrus ater
To 7 in. (18 cm)

European Starling
Sturnus vulgaris
To 8 in. (20 cm)

Blue Jay
Cyanocitta cristata
To 14 in. (35 cm)

Red-winged Blackbird
Agelaius phoeniceus
To 9 in. (23 cm)

Black-capped Chickadee
Poecile atricapillus
To 6 in. (15 cm)
Name-saying call is –
chick-a-dee-dee-dee.

White-breasted Nuthatch
Sitta carolinensis
To 6 in. (15 cm)

House Wren
Troglodytes aedon
To 5 in. (13 cm)

Eastern Meadowlark
Sturnella magna
To 9 in. (23 cm)

Eastern Bluebird
Sialia sialis
To 7 in. (18 cm)

American Robin
Turdus migratorius
To 11 in. (28 cm)
Wisconsin's state bird.

Brown Thrasher
Toxostoma rufum
To 12 in. (30 cm)

Dark-eyed Junco
Junco hyemalis
To 7 in. (18 cm)

Gray Catbird
Dumetella carolinensis
To 9 in. (23 cm)
Note black cap. Call has cat-like "mew" notes.

Baltimore Oriole
Icterus galbula
To 8 in. (20 cm)

Cedar Waxwing
Bombycilla cedrorum
To 7 in. (18 cm)
Red wing marks look like waxy droplets.

Eastern Towhee
Pipilo erythrophthalmus
To 9 in. (23 cm)
Cheerful song is –
drink-your-tea
or drink-tea.

House Sparrow
Passer domesticus
To 6 in. (15 cm)

Rose-breasted Grosbeak
Pheucticus ludovicianus
To 9 in. (23 cm)

American Goldfinch
Spinus tristis
To 5 in. (13 cm)

Purple Finch
Haemorhous purpureus
To 6 in. (15 cm)

Song Sparrow
Melospiza melodia
To 7 in. (18 cm)
Note central breast spot.

Northern Cardinal
Cardinalis cardinalis
To 9 in. (23 cm)

Virginia Opossum
Didelphis virginiana
To 40 in. (1 m)
Note long fur and naked tail.

Little Brown Bat
Myotis lucifugus
To 3.5 in. (9 cm)

Eastern Cottontail
Sylvilagus floridanus
To 18 in. (45 cm)

Eastern Chipmunk
Tamias striatus
To 12 in. (30 cm)
Note white stripes on side and face.

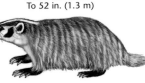

Red Squirrel
Tamiasciurus hudsonicus
To 14 in. (35 cm)

Thirteen-lined Ground Squirrel
Spermophilus tridecemlineatus
To 12 in. (30 cm)

Snowshoe Hare
Lepus americanus
To 20 in. (50 cm)
Coat is white in winter.

Eastern Gray Squirrel
Sciurus carolinensis
To 20 in. (50 cm)

Deer Mouse
Peromyscus maniculatus
To 8 in. (20 cm)
Distinguished by its white undersides and hairy tail.

Fox Squirrel
Sciurus niger
To 28 in. (70 cm)
Note large size and bushy tail. Largest squirrel in the US.

Northern Flying Squirrel
Glaucomys sabrinus
To 14 in. (35 cm)

House Mouse
Mus musculus To 8 in. (20 cm)
Introduced pest has a naked tail.

Woodchuck
Marmota monax
To 32 in. (80 cm)

Common Porcupine
Erethizon dorsatum To 3 ft. (90 cm)

Common Muskrat
Ondatra zibethicus
To 2 ft. (60 cm)
Aquatic rodent has a naked tail that is flattened on its sides.

Northern River Otter
Lontra canadensis
To 52 in. (1.3 m)

Mink
Neovison vison
To 28 in. (70 cm)
Chin is white.

American Badger
Taxidea taxus To 35 in. (88 cm)
Wisconsin's state animal.

Striped Skunk
Mephitis mephitis
To 32 in. (80 cm)

Red Fox
Vulpes vulpes To 40 in. (1 m)
Note white-tipped tail.

American Beaver
Castor canadensis
To 4 ft. (1.2 m)

Common Gray Fox
Urocyon cinereoargenteus
To 3.5 ft. (1.1 m)
Note black-tipped tail.

Common Raccoon
Procyon lotor
To 40 in. (1 m)

Bobcat
Lynx rufus To 4 ft. (1.2 m)

Coyote
Canis latrans
To 52 in. (1.3 m)
Note bushy, black-tipped tail.

Black Bear
Ursus americanus To 6 ft. (1.8 m)

White-tailed Deer
Odocoileus virginianus
To 7 ft. (2.1 m)
Wisconsin's state wildlife animal.

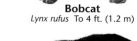